My First Spanish Book

KINGFISHER

KINGFISHER

Kingfisher Publications Plc
New Penderel House
283–288 High Holborn
London WC1V 7HZ
www.kingfisherpub.com

First published by Kingfisher Publications Plc 2007
2 4 6 8 10 9 7 5 3 1
Copyright © Kingfisher Publications Plc 2007
1TR/0207/WKT/PICA(PICA)/140MA/C

Illustrated by Mandy Stanley
Senior editor: Catherine Brereton
Senior designer: Malcolm Parchment
DTP manager: Nicky Studdart
Production controller: Teresa Wood

ISBN 978 0 7534 1438 5

Printed in China

Suggestions for parents

Sharing this book with your child is the ideal way to help him or her start the enjoyable journey of learning a foreign language. This bright, appealing book will establish the skills needed for confident learning and will act as an invaluable prompt for reading and becoming familiar with words in both English and Spanish.

Young children will enjoy browsing through the book, looking at the attractive pictures and reading and saying the words. Every picture shows a familiar object, labelled with its English word and its Spanish word in **bold**. This encourages an immediate association of Spanish word and object, so that young children can enjoy learning new Spanish words. It also encourages children to learn about the connection between an English word and its Spanish equivalent.

In Spanish, nouns (words for objects) are masculine or feminine. Instead of one word for 'the', as in English, Spanish uses **el** and **los** for masculine nouns and **la** and **las** for feminine nouns. **El** and **la** are singular, used if there is only one object. **Los** and **las** are plural, used if there is more than one object.

At the end of the book is a complete alphabetical list of all the Spanish words included in *My First Spanish Book*, along with a guide to how to say each word and some general hints about Spanish pronunciation.

Contents

Numbers 1 to 10
Los números del 1 al 10

1 one **uno**

2 two **dos**

3 three **tres**

4 four **cuatro**

5 five **cinco**

6 six **seis**

7 seven **siete**

8 eight **ocho**

9 nine **nueve**

10 ten **diez**

Numbers 11 to 20
Los números del 11 al 20

11 eleven
once

12 twelve
doce

13 thirteen
trece

14 fourteen
catorce

15 fifteen
quince

16 sixteen
dieciséis

6

17 seventeen
diecisiete

18 eighteen
dieciocho

19 nineteen
diecinueve

20 twenty
veinte

More numbers
Más números

30

thirty
treinta

40

forty
cuarenta

50

fifty
cincuenta

60

sixty
sesenta

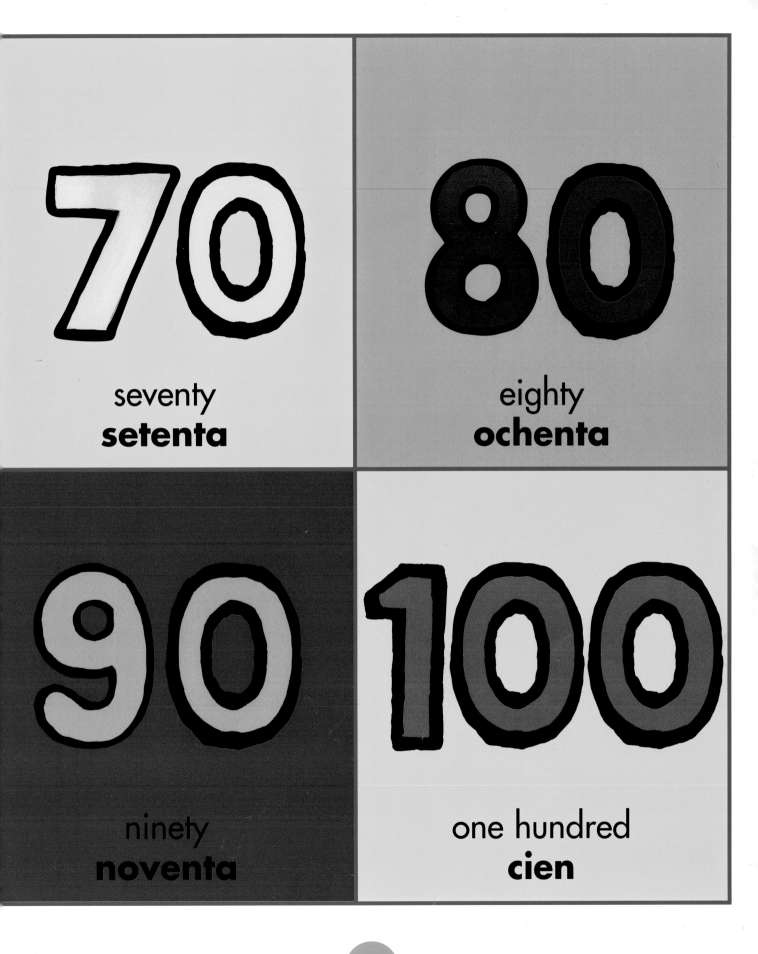

70
seventy
setenta

80
eighty
ochenta

90
ninety
noventa

100
one hundred
cien

Colours **Los colores**

black
negro

white
blanco

red
rojo

blue
azul

yellow
amarillo

purple
morado

green
verde

orange
naranja

pink
rosa

grey
gris

brown
marrón

11

Shapes **Las formas**

circle
el círculo

square
el cuadrado

triangle
el triángulo

rectangle
el rectángulo

diamond
el rombo

oval
el óvalo

star
la estrella

semi-circle
el semicírculo

13

Clothes **La ropa**

T-shirt
la camiseta

skirt
la falda

jeans
los vaqueros

gloves
los guantes

socks
los calcetínes

coat
el abrigo

jumper
el jersey

cap
la gorra

trainers
los zapatillas de deporte

shoes
los zapatos

belt
el cinturón

scarf
la bufanda

15

The body **El cuerpo**

nose
la nariz

toe
el dedo del pie

back
la espalda

chin
la barbilla

ear
la oreja

hair
el pelo

foot
el pie

hand
la mano

eye
el ojo

arm
el brazo

leg
la pierna

knee
la rodilla

Food **Los alimentos**

bread
el pan

pineapple
la piña

banana
el plátano

strawberry
la fresa

pie
el pastel

egg
el huevo

carrot
la zanahoria

ham
el jamón

cheese
el queso

orange
la naranja

apple
la manzana

ice lolly
el polo

19

The bedroom **El dormitorio**

teddy bear
el osito de peluche

ball
la pelota

pencil
el lápiz

pen
el bolígrafo

bed
la cama

lamp
la lámpara

yo-yo
el yoyó

carpet
la alfombra

comb
el peine

kite
la cometa

doll
la muñeca

book
el libro

21

The kitchen **La cocina**

fork
el tenedor

knife
el cuchillo

spoon
la cuchara

bowl
el tazón

plate
el plato

jar
el bote

cooker
la cocina

apron
el delantal

frying pan
la sartén

cup
la taza

The bathroom **El cuarto de baño**

bath
la bañera

duck
el pato

sponge
la esponja

towel
la toalla

basin
el lavabo

door
la puerta

mirror
el espejo

scales
la báscula

toothpaste
la pasta de dientes

soap
el jabón

toothbrush
el cepillo de dientes

The garden **El jardín**

butterfly
la mariposa

slug
la babosa

rake
el rastrillo

ant
la hormiga

ladybird
la mariquita

bird
el pájaro

gate
la puerta

spider's web
la telaraña

leaf
la hoja

nest
el nido

frog
la rana

worm
el gusano

The park **El parque**

pushchair
el carrito

dog
el perro

sandpit
el cajón de arena

rollerblades
los patines

flower
la flor

pond
el estanque

tricycle
el triciclo

tree
el árbol

swing
el columpio

slide
el tobogán

see-saw
el balancín

School **La escuela**

teacher
la maestra

table
la mesa

paints
las pinturas

paintbrush
el pincel

drawers
los cajones

backpack
la mochila

scissors
las tijeras

blocks
los bloques

chair
la silla

calculator
la calculadora

The supermarket **El supermercado**

milk
la leche

jam
la mermelada

trolley
el carrito

assistant
la dependienta

vegetables
las verduras

can
la lata

box
la caja

bag
la bolsa

till
la caja

fruit juice
el zumo

purse
el monedero

money
el dinero

The seaside **La playa**

starfish
la estrella de mar

sea
el mar

sandals
las sandalias

fish
el pez

yacht
el yate

crab
el cangrejo

sandcastle
el castillo de arena

spade
la pala

fishing net
la red

bucket
el cubo

shell
la concha

The farm **La granja**

tractor
el tractor

goat
la cabra

barn
el granero

pig
el cerdo

bull
el toro

36

house
la casa

chick
el pollito

calf
el ternero

sheep
la oveja

farmer
el granjero

cow
la vaca

cat
el gato

Animals **Los animales**

tiger
el tigre

wolf
el lobo

swan
el cisne

deer
el ciervo

monkey
el mono

parrot
el loro

bear
el oso

fox
el zorro

elephant
el elefante

seal
la foca

toucan
el tucán

zebra
la cebra

People **La gente**

woman
la mujer

girl
la niña

man
el hombre

boy
el niño

baby
el bebé

vet
el veterinario

chef
el cocinero

dancer
la bailarina

spy
el espía

dentist
la dentista

clown
el payaso

nurse
la enfermera

41

Transport **El transporte**

ship
el barco

rocket
el cohete

car
el coche

aeroplane
el avión

bus
el autobús

bicycle
la bicicleta

boat
la barca

lorry
el camión

motorbike
la moto

train
el tren

43

The weather **El tiempo**

sun
el sol

hail
el granizo

lightning
el rayo

fog
la niebla

rain
la lluvia

44

ice
el hielo

snow
la nieve

moon
la luna

cloud
la nube

wind
el viento

storm
la tormenta

45

Word list

In this list you will find all the Spanish words in this book, in **bold**. Next to each one is a guide to pronunciation (how to say it) and the English translation.

Remember that in Spanish, nouns (words for objects) are masculine or feminine. Instead of one word for 'the', as in English, Spanish uses **el** and **los** for masculine nouns and **la** and **las** for feminine nouns. **El** and **la** are singular, used if there is only one object. **Los** and **las** are plural, used if there is more than one object.

Some pronunciation tips

• Most Spanish words have a part that you stress, or say more strongly (like the 'loh' in 'colores'). The part of the word that you should stress is underlined in the guide, like this: koh-loh-ress.

• When you see 'rr' in the pronunciation guide, you should make a rolled 'r' sound, made by flapping your tongue against the roof of your mouth.

• When you see the letter 'r' at the beginning of a word in the pronunciation guide, you should say it as a rolled 'r' sound (as above).

• When you see the letter 'g' in the pronunciation guide, you should say it like the 'g' in the English word 'garden', not like the 'g' in the English word 'gentle'.

• A few Spanish words are said differently in different parts of the world. The pronunciations given here are for the usual pronunciation in Spain. An example is the word 'cinco', pronounced 'theen-ko'. In South America, the 'c' is pronounced differently, as 'seen-ko'.

abc

el abrigo	(el ah-bree-go)	coat
la alfombra	(la al-fom-brah)	carpet
los alimentos	(loss alee-men-toss)	food
amarillo	(a-mah-reel-yo)	yellow
los animales	(loss a-nee-mah-lees)	animals
el árbol	(el ar-bol)	tree
el autobús	(el ah-oo-toh-booss)	bus
el avión	(el ah-bee-on)	aeroplane
azul	(ah-thool)	blue
la babosa	(la bah-boh-ssa	slug
la bailarina	(la bay-la-ree-nah)	dancer
el balancín	(el bah-lan-than)	see-saw
la bañera	(la ban-yair-ah)	bath
la barbilla	(la bar-beel-yah)	chin
la barca	(la bar-kah)	boat
el barco	(el bar-koh)	ship
la bascula	(la bass-koo-lah)	scales
el bebé	(el bay-bay)	baby
la bicicleta	(la bee-thee-klay-ta)	bicycle
blanco	(blan-ko)	white
los bloques	(loss bloh-kayss)	blocks
el bolígrafo	(el boh-lee-grah-foh)	pen
la bolsa	(la bol-sa)	bag
el bote	(el boh-tay)	jar
el brazo	(el bra-tho)	arm
la bufanda	(la boo-fan-da)	scarf
la cabra	(la kah-bra)	goat
la caja	(la kah-ha)	box or till
el cajón de arena	(el kah-hon day ah-ray-na)	sandpit
los cajones	(loss kah-hoh-ness)	drawers
los calcetines	(loss kal-the-tee-ness)	socks
la calculadora	(la kal-koola-dor-ah)	calculator
la cama	(la kah-ma)	bed
el camión	(el kah-mee-on)	lorry
la camiseta	(la kah-mee-say-tah)	T-shirt
el cangrejo	(el kan-gray-ho)	crab
el carrito	(el ka-rree-toh)	trolley or pushchair
la casa	(la kah-sah)	house
el castillo de arena	(el kah-steel-yo day ah-ray-nah) sandcastle	
catorce	(kah-tor-thay)	fourteen
la cebra	(la thay-brah)	zebra
el cepillo de dientes	(el thay-peel-yo day dee-en-tess) toothbrush	
el cerdo	(el thair-doh)	pig
cien	(thee-en)	a hundred
el ciervo	(el thee-ayr-boh)	deer
cinco	(theen-koh)	five
cincuenta	(theen-kwen-ta)	fifty
el cinturón	(el theen-too-ron)	belt
el círculo	(el theer-koo-loh)	circle
el cisne	(el thiss-nay)	swan
el coche	(el koh-chay)	car
la cocina	(la ko-thee-nah)	cooker or kitchen

el cocinero (el ko-thee-<u>nair</u>-oh)	chef	
el cohete (el koh-<u>ay</u>-tay)	rocket	
los colores (loss koh-<u>loh</u>-ress)	colours	
el columpio (el koh-<u>loom</u>-pee-oh)	swing	
la cometa (la koh-<u>may</u>-tah)	kite	
la concha (la <u>kon</u>-chah)	shell	
el cuadrado (el kwa-<u>drah</u>-doh)	square	
cuarenta (kwa-<u>ren</u>-ta)	forty	
el cuarto de baño (el <u>kwar</u>-toh day <u>ban</u>-yo)	bathroom	
cuatro (<u>kwa</u>-troh)	four	
el cubo (el <u>koo</u>-boh)	bucket	
la cuchara (la koo-<u>cha</u>-rrah)	spoon	
el cuchillo (el koo-<u>cheel</u>-yo)	knife	
el cuerpo (el <u>kwair</u>-poh)	body	

def

el dedo del pie (el <u>day</u>-do del <u>pee</u>-ay)	toe
el delantal (el de-lan-<u>tal</u>)	apron
la dentista (la den-<u>tees</u>-tah)	dentist
la dependienta (la de-pen-dee-<u>en</u>-tah)	assistant (in a shop)
diecinueve (dee-ay-thee-<u>nwe</u>-bay)	nineteen
dieciocho (dee-ay-thee-<u>o</u>-cho)	eighteen
diecisiete (dee-ay-thee-see-<u>e</u>-tay)	seventeen
dieciséis (dee-ay-thee-<u>says</u>)	sixteen
diez (dee-<u>eth</u>)	ten
el dinero (el dee-<u>nair</u>-oh)	money
doce (<u>do</u>-thay)	twelve
el dormitorio (el dor-mee-<u>toh</u>-<u>rree</u>-oh)	bedroom
dos (doss)	two

el elefante (el e-lay-<u>fan</u>-tay)	elephant
la enfermera (la en-fayr-<u>mayr</u>-ah)	nurse
la escuela (la ess-<u>kway</u>-lah)	school
la espalda (la ess-<u>pal</u>-dah)	back
el espejo (el ess-<u>pay</u>-hoh)	mirror
el espía (el ess-<u>pee</u>-ah)	spy
la esponja (la ess-<u>pon</u>-ha)	sponge
el estanque (el ess-<u>tan</u>-kay)	pond
la estrella (la ess-<u>trel</u>-yah)	star
la estrella de mar (la ess-<u>trel</u>-yahh day mar)	starfish

la falda (la <u>fal</u>-dah)	skirt
la flor (la flor)	flower
la foca (la <u>foh</u>-ka)	seal
las formas (lass <u>for</u>-mass)	shapes
la fresa (la <u>fre</u>-ssah)	strawberry

ghi

el gato (el <u>gah</u>-to)	cat
la gente (la <u>hayn</u>-tay)	people
la gorra (la <u>goh</u>-rra)	cap
el granero (el grah-<u>nay</u>-ro)	barn
el granizo (el grah-<u>nee</u>-thoh)	hail
la granja (la <u>gran</u>-ha)	farm
el granjero (el gran-<u>hay</u>-ro)	farmer
gris (<u>greess</u>)	grey

los guantes (loss <u>gwan</u>-tays)	gloves
el gusano (el goo-<u>sah</u>-noh)	worm

el hielo (el ee-<u>ay</u>-loh)	ice
la hoja (la <u>oh</u>-ha)	leaf
el hombre (el <u>om</u>-bray)	man
la hormiga (la or-<u>mee</u>-gah)	ant
el huevo (el <u>woo</u>-ay-boh)	egg

jkl

el jabón (el ha-<u>bon</u>)	soap
el jamón (el ha-<u>mon</u>)	ham
el jardín (el har-<u>deen</u>)	garden
el jersey (el hair-say)	jersey

la lámpara (la <u>lam</u>-pah-rah)	lamp
el lapiz (el <u>lah</u>-peeth)	pencil
la lata (la <u>lah</u>-tah)	tin
el lavabo (el <u>lah</u>-bah-boh)	basin
la leche (la <u>lay</u>-chay)	milk
el libro (el <u>lee</u>-broh)	book
la lluvia (la <u>yoo</u>-bee-ah)	rain
el lobo (el <u>loh</u>-boh)	wolf
el loro (el <u>loh</u>-roh)	parrot
la luna (la <u>loo</u>-nah)	moon

mn

la maestra (la mah-<u>ays</u>-trah)	teacher (primary school)
la mano (la <u>mah</u>-noh)	hand
la manzana (la man-<u>tha</u>-nah)	apple
el mar (el <u>mar</u>)	sea
la mariposa (la mah-ree-<u>poh</u>-ssa)	butterfly
la mariquita (la mah-ree-<u>kee</u>-ta)	ladybird
marrón (mah-<u>rron</u>)	brown
la mermelada (la mair-may-<u>lah</u>-dah)	jam
la mesa (la <u>may</u>-sah)	table
la mochila (la moh-<u>chee</u>-lah)	backpack
el monedero (el moh-nay-<u>day</u>-rroh)	purse
el mono (el <u>moh</u>-noh)	monkey
morado (moh-<u>rah</u>-doh)	purple
la moto (la <u>moh</u>-toh)	motorbike
la mujer (la moo-<u>hair</u>)	woman
la muñeca (la moo-<u>nyay</u>-kah)	doll

naranja (nah-<u>ran</u>-ha)	orange (colour)
la naranja (la nah-<u>ran</u>-ha)	orange (fruit)
la nariz (la nah-riz)	nose
negro (<u>nay</u>-gro)	black
el nido (el <u>nee</u>-doh)	nest
la niebla (la nee-<u>ay</u>-blah)	fog
la nieve (la nee-<u>ay</u>-bah)	snow
la niña (la <u>nee</u>-nya)	girl
el niño (el <u>nee</u>-nyo)	boy
noventa (noh-<u>bayn</u>-tah)	ninety
la nube (la <u>noo</u>-bay)	cloud

nueve (nwe-bay) — nine
los números (loss noo-may-ross) — numbers

op

ochenta (oh-chen-tah) — eighty
ocho (oh-choh) — eight
el ojo (el oh-hoh) — eye
once (on-thay) — eleven
la oreja (la oh-re-ha) — ear
el osito de peluche (el os-see-to day pe-loo-chay) — teddy bear
el oso (el os-so) — bear
el óvalo (el oh-bah-loh) — oval
la oveja (la oh-be-ha) — sheep

el pájaro (el pa-haro) — bird
el pan (el pan) — bread
la pala (la pa-lah) — spade
el parque (el par-kay) — park
la pasta de dientes (la pass-ta day dee-en-tess) — toothpaste
el pastel (el pass-tel) — pie
los patines (loss pa-tee-nes) — rollerblades
el pato (el pah-toh) — duck
el payaso (el pah-yah-so) — clown
el peine (el pay-nay) — comb
el pelo (el pe-loh) — hair
la pelota (la pe-lot-ah) — ball
el perro (el pay-rroh) — dog
el pez (el peth) — fish
el pie (el pee-ay) — foot
la pierna (la pee-ayr-nah) — leg
el pincel (el peen-thel) — paintbrush
la piña (la pee-nya) — pineapple
las pinturas (lass peen-too-rass) — paints
el plátano (el plah-tah-noh) — banana
el plato (el plah-toh) — plate
la playa (la plah-yah) — beach
el pollito (el poh-lyee-toh) — chick
el polo (el poh-loh) — ice lolly
la puerta (la pwair-tah) — door or gate

qrs

el queso (el kay-ssoh) — cheese
quince (keen-thay) — fifteen

la rana (la rah-nah) — frog
el rastrillo (el ras-treel-yo) — rake
el rayo (el rah-yo) — lightning
el rectángulo (el rec-tan-goo-loh) — rectangle
la red (la rayd) — fishing net
la rodilla (la roh-deel-yah) — knee
rojo (roh-ho) — red
el rombo (el rom-bo) — diamond
la ropa (la roh-pah) — clothes
rosa (roh-ssah) — pink

las sandalias (lass san-dah-lee-yas) — sandals
la sartén (la sar-ten) — frying pan
seis (sayss) — six
el semicírculo (el se-mee-theer-koo-loh) — semi-circle
sesenta (se-sen-tah) — sixty
setenta (se-ten-tah) — seventy
siete (see-e-tay) — seven
la silla (la seel-ya) — chair
el sol (el sol) — sun
el supermercado (el soo-per-mer-kah-doh) — supermarket

tu

la taza (la tah-tha) — cup
el tazón (el tah-thon) — bowl
la telaraña (la te-lah-ran-ya) — spider's web
el tenedor (el te-ne-dor) — fork
el ternero (el tayr-nay-ro) — calf
el tiempo (el tee-em-poh) — weather
el tigre (el tee-gray) — tiger
las tijeras (lass tee-hay-rass) — scissors
la toalla (la toh-al-ya) — towel
el toboggan (el toh-boh-gan) — slide
la tormenta (la tor-men-tah) — storm
el toro (el toh-roh) — bull
el tractor (el trak-tor) — tractor
el transporte (el tran-spor-tay) — transport
trece (tre-thay) — thirteen
treinta (trayn-tah) — thirty
el tren (el tren) — train
tres (tress) — three
el triángulo (el tree-an-goo-loh) — triangle
el triciclo (el tree-thee-kloh) — tricycle
el tucán (el too-kan) — toucan

uno (oo-no) — one

vw

la vaca (la bah-kah) — cow
los vaqueros (loss bah-kay-ross) — jeans
veinte (bayn-tay) — twenty
verde (bair-day) — green
las verduras (lass bair-doo-rays) — vegetables
el veterinario (el be-tay-ree-nah-ree-oh) — vet
el viento (el bee-en-toh) — wind

xyz

el yate (el yah-tay) — yacht
el yoyó (el yo-yo) — yo-yo

la zanahoria (la tha-nah-or-ee-ah) — carrot
los zapatillas (los tha-pah-teel-yas) — shoes
los zapatillas de deporte (los tha-pah-teel-yas day de-por-tay) — trainers
el zorro (el tho-rroh) — fox
el zumo (el thoo-moh) — fruit juice